James Billings

The *UN*CORPORATION

Unleashing the Power
of the Business Trust
for Your Protection and Privacy

TrustArte™
Asset Privacy • Trust Strategies

The *Un*corporation: Unleashing the Power of the Business
Trust for Your Protection and Privacy

Author: James Billings
Co-author and book design: Victor Hernandez
James Billings's portrait by Robb Carr

Cover image: The Rockefeller-Morgan Family Tree by John
Moody 1904 public domain

www.trustarte.com
www.trustartesolutions.com

ISBN-13: 978-1-7322048-1-2
ISBN-10: 1-7322048-1-0
First Edition. 2018. San Diego, California USA
Published by TA Media Trust

CreateSpace, a DBA of On-Demand Publishing, LLC
Charleston, SC USA
www.createspace.com

TABLE OF CONTENTS

About the Author   vii

Dedication   ix

Preface   xi

Introduction   1

Fair Warning / House Rules   5

Chapter 1:

    The Story of James   9

Chapter 2:

    Traditional Business Structures   17

Chapter 3:

    What is a Business Trust   27

Chapter 4:

    Banking and Taxes with a Business Trust   33

Chapter 5:

    More Benefits of a Business Trust   43

Chapter 6:

    The Components of a Business Trust   57

Chapter 7:

    What Can I do with a Business Trust   65

Chapter 8:

    What Types of Trust are There   69

Chapter 9:

    Reactive and Proactive   77

Chapter 10:

    How do I Set up a Business Trust?   85

Epilogue: What Lawyers Won't Tell You   91

Acknowledgments   95

Glossary   97

Bibliography   107

Index   109

ABOUT THE AUTHOR

James Billings

James is a global businessman. His professional credentials and success both touch valuable assets such as real estate, aircraft and businesses. Years ago he recognized the danger of internet search to "pull back the curtain" on your financial privacy. Today he provides solutions for clients who want their assets to remain unlisted or invisible. The key is "title" anonymity. James lives in San Diego and Buenos Aires.

This book is dedicated to Paul and Efrain

- James Billings

PREFACE

The genesis of this book originated in the early 90's with a man named Richard. He advised me to not look for what is there but for what is *missing* from the picture. A few years later Jack introduced the concept of title *privacy* for real estate assets themselves.

In the following twenty years the "world wide web" revolutionized access to valuable financial data. It has rendered corporations and LLCs obsolete for asset anonymity. Given human nature we know this is dangerous because people use our information against us and even for illegal purposes. We read about it in the news every day.

My solution to asset privacy is unlisted ownership using "title" strategies. Rather than a registered corporation or LLC, we use a trust instrument. It's a proven old tool adapted to our new internet world.

As a business professional I've sought to keep financial affairs confidential as do most people. I helped investor clients achieve similar results. It never occurred to me to write a book until a few years ago.

You might be skeptical because very few know how. However, it is undisputed that a trust can, if designed properly, ensure asset privacy. It works for a bank account, real estate, or your business. Consider it a "privacy curtain" for your assets.

What's been *missing* is education on how to get these results from our standard resources. I am now here to share with you concepts, experiences, applications, strategies and solutions for those who choose asset *privacy*. This book will walk you through how it all works.

INTRODUCTION

For many years we've been told that if we want to do business we need to have a company structured as a corporation or as a LLC. And we just take it for granted. We file the paperwork with the state government, we pay fees, and we pay taxes. What they don't tell us is traditional business structures, such as corporations and LLCs, actually have very big and very real risks and disadvantages to ourselves, to our property, to our privacy and to our money.

They also don't tell us there is an alternative, more flexible, simpler way to do business that does not require governmental registration, nor fees, taxes or any of the expenses associated with registering a traditional business corporation or LLC. State government officials and many legal experts have no incentive to tell you about alternative business models. Furthermore, they don't really know what I'm about to share with you. Since They can lose money if people don't conform to traditional business structures, they have no real reason to say anything about it.

INTRODUCTION

Additionally, this alternative business structure can protect your privacy, your assets and your money in ways traditional business structures can't. This alternative business structure is known as the business trust. I call it the *un*corporation.

And guess what? While we have been taught to passively file paperwork, pay tons of money, and go through lots of rules and regulations in order to do business, for over a century mega-rich families like the Rockefellers, the Carnegies, the Kennedys, the Murdochs, and even the Waltons from Walmart and Sam's Club, do not use just traditional business structures to operate their businesses, but a variety of business structures that include business trusts in order to manage their wealth. They strategically use business trusts in order to provide their own wealth and businesses a privacy curtain and a level of protection most people have not even though they could. This is possible with far less effort and expenses than setting up a corporation or LLC.

A business trust is a formal business structure that also includes business banking and can be completely invisible to outsiders and operated without the Secretary of State. Business trusts are used by companies and wealthy people in the USA, UK, Australia, Hong Kong, Singapore, Japan and India. Trillions of dollars in assets are handled through these commercial business trusts.

Ask yourself the following questions: Are you a business

2

owner sensitive to the privacy of your assets and your money? Do you want the entire world to know what you own and how much money you have? Are you weary of state government regulations and financial theft from litigation? If the answer is yes, then this book is for you.

However, if you have the money to have a team of lawyers on speed dial, you dismiss the significance of asset privacy, and you feel immune to life's financial surprises than maybe this book is not for you. But if you do care for your privacy, you understand how a breach of your financial privacy can obliterate you and your family (especially in the internet era of identity theft and even corporate identity theft), and you understand how priceless is the peace of mind that comes with the knowledge that your business and your wealth are secure, then this book is for you. So come on. Let's learn how to *un*corporate.

INTRODUCTION

FAIR WARNING/ HOUSE RULES

This book is not legal, tax or accounting advice. This is information based on my personal experience of 23 years working with 'trusts' for holding title to assets. This book translates esoteric academic essays and legal summaries along with my personal experiences to bring you a simple understanding in plain English of how a business trust works and its benefits. It is for educational purposes only. For actual legal or accounting advice please consult your own professional adviser, but never take anybody's opinion about the rules at face value. You want to see page, chapter and verse. If you've got a transaction, if you've got taxes, if you've got legal issues you really owe it to yourself to understand what some of the important criteria are. You don't need to drill down into super deep but you do need to understand the basics of how these things work.

If there's a question for you, ask your lawyer, ask your

accountant "where is that rule? Let me see it in the Civil Code. Let me see it in procedures. Let me see in the Internal Revenue Code. Let me look it up." It's not that difficult to do. It just takes a few minutes a reading. Once you internalize some of these things it really changes your strategic outlook on how you want to get things done. Because the two most dangerous words in the world are, "they said." So never take anyone's opinion at face value. Always look up stuff. Read the rules, read the code, read the law. Ask for details and be aware of the factual information behind somebody's opinion in order to better evaluate it. Read also about possible penalties for not following the rules, codes and laws. If you don't do this, then that will happen. If you do that, then this will happen.

Also, do not pay anyone to do your thinking for you. Ask professionals for tactical advice, but do your own thinking and establish what you want to do instead of letting others do it for you.

Finally, please read the section on possible handicaps so you can be fully aware of the advantages and disadvantages presented in this book. You will find that the possible handicaps are so small compared to the benefits that they may not even seem like handicaps at all. But you do need to be aware of them.

Keep in mind this book is about education. I am sharing knowledge, strategies and practical applications. It provides information that is useful, valuable, and that will make you a more informed person in regards to business structures. You will see comparisons of different business structures, what their features are and how they can benefit you or work against you.

FAIR WARNING/HOUSE RULES

CHAPTER 1

THE STORY OF JAMES

Businessman Pilot

My name is James Billings. I earned professional credentials in both the securities and real estate industry. During nearly three decades of handling transactions for clients, they often asked me about tax and title strategies. "James, how do we hold title for maximum privacy?" A mentor taught me the best way to create anonymity for assets. It was neither a corporation or an LLC. As a result, I'm now known as an expert on "Title and Situs" for asset privacy. Sophisticated clients these days really prefer anonymous title.

We'll talk more in detail about Title and Situs which refers to ownership and location of assets later in the book. No I'm not a lawyer. I advise clients buying and selling valuable assets. They are all concerned about legal title. So I cultivated this niche expertise to add depth for a client's peace of mind. I specifically use trust instruments to design a "privacy curtain" for legal title to your assets. It could be real estate, a bank account or a business.

Before we get further into my business credentials I'd like to share my pilot story. My first lesson was in 1970 and I went on to earn an FAA Commercial Pilot's Certificate plus various ratings. The reason for this mention is because when you're in flight school, you are trained to plan and think ahead. To create a flight plan you must, first know your destination, how much fuel you will need, the weather conditions, which airport you're going to land, how much weight you will be carrying, and other pieces of information that you must know in order to arrive to your destination safely. If you fail to plan ahead, you increase the risk of an off airport landing or worse. Remember, the pilot always hits first.

That's how I approach business; Always planning ahead. Always thinking about the possible contingencies and always personalizing business plans. That is very important when you want to *un*corporate, as we will see later in the book.

My father died when I was 15 years old. He was flying an RA5C Vigilante which malfunctioned and 'bought the farm.' But I've always loved airplanes. As a teenager I had a line job at the small general aviation airport. I've always been around airplanes all my life. I graduated college by earning a degree in economics from Pepperdine up in

Malibu, California. I have also always enjoyed business.

Afterwards, I became a successful stockbroker, corporate pilot, and real estate broker. Each pursuit always involved buying and selling valuable assets. So over those years my clients and myself had exposure to sole proprietors, partnerships, general partnerships, limited partnerships, corporations, and LLCs. We used those standard structures with the accountants and lawyers in the traditional way.

Working with traditional business structures allowed me to realize they had important defects. One main frustration with corporations and LLCs was the public visibility factor. By that I mean this: when you set up a traditional business structure, such as a corporation or an LLC, the information on its principals, becomes visible. By law this Secretary of State information has to be available to the public. In the internet era, starting in the 1990s, that meant anyone can look into your business information (names, addresses, dates) from anywhere in the world. What if somebody uses the information against you? Say, to sue you, or to try to get your property. Or even to steal your corporate identity and do fraudulent transactions on your corporation's name without you even knowing about it. Plus, corporations carry the risk of what is known as "piercing the corporate veil." That is, the financial and liability protections that corporations are supposed to protect you as an individual can simply disappear if you do not follow several cumbersome rules and regulations.

The Trust, the Meltdown, and the Realization

In 1995 I was introduced to a new device for holding title to assets (that is, legal ownership) and one of its main benefits was privacy. A fascinating businessman and mentor named Jack Miller introduced me to this for real estate. The device is also known as a 'land' trust which is a rather narrow term given it's full capabilities. We began using these trusts for holding real estate. Other types of trusts were used for my aircraft, business, property management companies and then also for bank accounts. You can use the basic trust instrument for different types of assets. Trusts can have many different designs and thus purposes which we'll talk about later. But the 'anonymous' title aspect was really quite special.

While I'm having practical experiences with this new type of title holding trusts, the rest of life goes on and am involved with investments in real estate. But in 2010, after the financial crisis, I had my ultimate meltdown. I was sued by a real estate investor. I have never been poor but I was temporarily broke. I was down flat on my back, and $850,000 in debt. I lost my airplane too. I just felt like "take me." A number of my real estate mentors had died including Jack. I had family members and close friends who died. That means about seven or eight people dying. It was just all crap. I just broke loose at once.

Rolling around trying to figure out what to do to get back on my feet I started thinking. With all this experience I've got with business and finance, what's missing from our financial education and from professional advisers? What can I offer to the world that's highly valuable and not really available to most people? And what I realized was it was all about how to title your assets for privacy and safety. I realized I knew how to teach people to secure their assets so they would be private and safe. That's what I'd offer to the world, how to put a "privacy curtain" in front of your assets.

Although I've been using the real estate and business trusts for years, I never really thought about them as a business. I just did it for my own stuff and for clients. But when you stop to look at it there's really no guidance from lawyers or stockbrokers or real estate brokers on how to do it. When they ask you about title, you generally just think of your own personal name, tenants in common, joint tenants, or maybe there's a corporation or LLC. But where's the privacy strategy? Most people don't know. Most barely know that "title" is the legal concept of ownership of an asset.

On top of that, there's little effort from lawyers, stock brokers and real estate brokers about issues of title privacy because generally their only focus is to facilitate a single transaction. It could be buying or selling a property, opening a brokerage account or selecting a business structure. They're unable to look at your entire portfolio and make recommendations about title and situs because they don't focus on the entire picture. They focus on a single frame of your movie. And they don't look at the entire movie because that's not what they do. It's the opposite of a holistic approach. It's not part of their assignment, if you will. Plus, they operate with the default mindset of traditional corporate structures, not with business trusts.

Even worse; many people don't know corporations and LLC involve *visible* title because those are their default attributes. But with a business trust you can get *invisible* title benefits by design, thus giving you a privacy curtain and peace of mind in the knowledge that strangers can't get to your private asset information from the Secretary of State. I would advise and teach people how to use trusts in order to get those title benefits that offer privacy and that peace of mind.

A couple of years later I knew life had to get better and I realized that all these trust title transactions were tremendously valuable. The knowledge about real estate and business trusts is actually a scarce resource. Furthermore, I had applied this knowledge in many transactions. I made tons of mistakes too. This self-initiated expertise was something that I had cultivated and developed. I knew I could help a lot of other people.

Professional advisors are not really into this space. I realized that securing privacy for "title vesting" is really, really scarce information. It just really hasn't been addressed before. It's missing. So I went on to truly dig deep into researching business, real estate and other forms of trusts.

My historical research became fascinating when I went to the archives of the Vatican Library and American Academy in Rome to learn about the origins of trusts. It was then described as fideicommissa (Latin) and principally used by wealth citizens of Rome to pass on a personal estate. Another version developed in the Middle Ages for real property in the UK. A third version was implemented for businesses in the USA.

Again, lawyers have zero incentive to explain title privacy. They need transparency to find your assets. As we will see later in the book, if anything lawyers have two main incentives not to explain title privacy and how to get it. So the careful question is, ignorance or lack of integrity? Asset privacy is a big deal. It's one of the foundations for safety of your property. It's also human nature. But almost nobody makes the effort to make sure people understand that and how much safer their assets are with real estate or business privacy.

What I do is I take a holistic approach to advising my clients. I look at the entire movie (portfolio) instead of looking at a single frame (transaction) like most lawyers and brokers. I explain how they can re-title their assets with private trusts without tax consequences. You can use an existing corporation or LLC as the beneficiary if that's their preference. Being able to see the entire movie gives me a different perspective to recognize the exposed assets.

So my clients said one day "hey, James, what if you create course or write a book on trusts?" Yes. It would be so much easier because one of the things that happens when I'm helping them out is that they always ask different questions about title and trusts. We always end up looking up different fragments of information from the entire title ecosystem. What if I could simply unify the information into a concise course showing people what a business trust is and how it can secure the title of your property so you can have a privacy curtain and peace of mind?

That is what this book is about.

But with an important distinction. This book is not just about explaining business trusts and asset privacy. It's also about rethinking the way you plan how to do business. Shift from defense to offense. Change your mindset so you plan ahead and use trusts for business with a strategic design in mind. That is, to help you design the way you will secure your assets for maximum privacy.

In other words, to teach you how to *un*corporate.

CHAPTER 2

TRADITIONAL BUSINESS STRUCTURES

The Risks of the Traditional Business Structures

Most people don't realize there are tremendous risks to their assets when they do business with traditional business structures. These traditional business structures include corporations, LLCs, Partnerships, Sole Proprietors, etc. They all have two facts in common. One: They must be registered with a government called the Secretary of State, and/or get a business license from the city or county in the case of Sole Proprietors, which is also a form of government registration. Two: As a result of the registration with the Secretary of State, or the license with the city or county with Sole Proprietors, their information must be available to the public which is online. Shareholders and stockholders may be confidential and therefore not immediately visible to outsiders, but the business 'itself' is visible to pretty much anyone, which is a big risk to the shareholders and stockholders, as we will see later.

This means three things. *One*: If you want to do business in the United States you have to spend money, time and resources filing paperwork and paying fees and taxes in order to have *permission* from the state government to have the *privilege* of doing business (we'll get into detail about this in a bit). *Two*: If you fail to follow all of the rules and regulations you can lose the legal protections from having a corporation. *Three*: Once you register the corporation, or LLC, or Partnership, or etc with the Secretary of State, your business information (personal names, address, phone numbers, dates, etc.) becomes available in public databases anyone can search from anywhere in the world through the internet.

Let's take a look at each of these items in detail.

The Red Tape Risk

Say you want to have a company in California. You want to register a company because you want a corporate banking account and the various benefits that come with having a corporation. That means you will have to do all of the following in order to get your company registered and keep it registered:

1. Hire a lawyer or do the paperwork yourself.

2. Pick a name for your company that's not already taken in the Secretary of State registration database. You pay to reserve that name for 60 days.

3. File initial paperwork with the Secretary of State.

4. Pay the fees for the registration with the Secretary of State.

5. Wait weeks for the approval of the paperwork. If there's an error in your paperwork, you have to wait even longer.

6. File a statement of information within 6 months.

7. Pay franchise taxes every year. The franchise tax is a tax paid for the privilege of doing business in a state.

8. Name and pay for a Resident Agent who will be receiving service of process (legal action notices.)

9. Identify your Company Officers and Directors.

10. Hold shareholder meetings, record the minutes of the meetings in writing, and have them available for inspection if challenged.

11. Hold officer meetings, recordkeeping of other information on company business recorded such as banking resolutions from director meetings.

12. Spend time and money required to maintain all of the above year after year.

By the way; the minimum franchise tax for a

corporation in California is $800 or 8.8% of the company income per year, whichever one is greater, even if your business doesn't make any money. The fee for the Secretary of State registration is $100 per year, while the fee for a Resident Agent is $150. In other words, you will have to pay at least $1,050 per year in order to have a business in California even if you don't make any profits from it. And you could easily spend another $750 for a lawyer just to do this setup.

Multiply just the franchise tax over five years of operating your business. That's $4,000 out of your pocket. For people with a lot of money that may not a big deal, but for thrifty businesses that can be a lot of money.

And if you want to have more than one corporation or LLC, you will have to start from square one and pay a new set of fees and taxes for each new corporation registered with the Secretary of State. Again you might also pay for lawyers to do your paperwork and filings. Multiply this by the number of years your company will operate and that's a lot of money over time spent out of your pocket even if you have zero revenues at the start. Not only that; if you want to do business in another state, you have to register your corporation (or "naturalize it") in that state, meaning you have to do all the paperwork, pay the fees and the taxes for the new state as well. In other words, more red tape and more money spent just to do business. Are you game?

The Corporate Veil Piercing Risk

The 'corporate veil' is the term used to describe the legal benefits and protections you can get when you use a traditional corporate structure. For example: in case of a lawsuit against your company, the company is responsible for the lawsuit, not you personally. But if you fail to follow the rules and regulations set by the state for corporations, you can lose the legal benefits and protections, thus rendering you personally responsible for a lawsuit against your company. This is known as piercing the corporate veil, the alter ego doctrine. This generally occurs when the organization is sued because they're either unable or unwilling to make a payment.

If the corporate veil is pierced, any attack against your business can also become a personal attack against you and against your personal property. A lawsuit against your company could lead to you losing your personal property, bank accounts, and other assets, as the legal and liability protections from the corporate veil will no longer protect you. Not to mention the damage to your personal credit report and financial standing.

It gets worse. If the corporate veil is pierced, your company contracts can be voided. Let's say one of your providers is giving you a really big bulk discount in a futures contract you signed with the provider. If perhaps the corporate veil is pierced in a dispute with that provider,

21

the contract discount can be voided after legal proceedings. You're now subject to the current market pricing which could be significant to your bottom line.

If your company files for bankruptcy and the veil is pierced creditors can pursue the owners personal assets for payment or get a judgment.

If tax authorities pierce the veil they can recast all corporate 1120 earnings taxes to much higher personal 1040 rates with interest and penalties back to the beginning.

Guess what? If you neglect to hold stockholder meetings and keep record of the minutes of the meetings, you can lose the corporate veil. Not only that; if you do not hold shareholder meetings, even if there's only one shareholder in the company (you), you may have trouble selling the company later on, as potential buyers may want to look at detailed corporate records and avoid buying a company without required records.

If you fail to keep the company officers and a resident agent (and of course pay their salaries/fees), you can jeopardize the corporate veil. If you do not pay the franchise tax, you can lose the corporate veil. The major point here is your personal assets can be vulnerable.

If your company sues someone and you lose the veil, you can lose all legal standing in court.

For a big, multinational corporation like Google, Amazon, Apple, General Electric or Walmart, this may not look like a big deal, because they have in-house staff lawyers to ensure the veil remains intact. But if you are a small company, piercing the corporate veil can be devastating. If you are an independent business owner who spends his time running your company, this can be a huge problem, because it will pull your attention and resources from running the company and it will force you to focus on litigation and other defensive issues that come with lifting the corporate veil. You've read about these stories in the news.

Do you fully understand how big a burden you would be taking by using a traditional corporate structure?

The Public Information Risk

Once you register a traditional corporation with the Secretary of State, your business is visible. Outsiders may not be able to see who the shareholders or stockholders are, but they will see the business filing information (names, physical address, phone, email, etc.) and the Resident Agent. This makes your business a visible target for lawsuits if somebody tries to find a way to sue your business for the sake of profit. This is a really big problem in the internet era.

It gets worse; there have been cases of thieves stealing valuable property by changing the data on a company registered on the Secretary of State's database. It works like this: Thief searches Secretary of State and real property records. If they find a Corporation or LLC that owns valuable real estate, it's a ripe match. Thief then files a change of manager or officer to a nominee. Nominee then takes out a loan or sells your business real estate. And they do this simply by changing data in the Secretary of State's website.

In the past, before the internet era, if somebody wanted to know the information of a corporation, that person would have to go in person or US Mail to the Secretary of State office and look up the physical record. If the person lived in a different state, he might face an even bigger challenge in order to look up the information. In other words, it was a cumbersome, impractical task. This also applies to bank account searches. But with the introduction of the internet, that same business information that used to be cumbersome and impractical to find out is now found simply by using Google. If you have a business and you type the name on Google, is the official information for the business registered with the Secretary of State going to come up? Most likely, yes.

"Why is this a problem? I have nothing to hide," some may say. Actually, you do have something to hide: Your financial assets privacy.

Let's say a vendor or employee wants to sue your company. For whatever reason, real or fantasy. The mindset is "well, a corporation has money, right? Let's find a way to sue it and get some of their money." Sometimes lawsuits are filed without merit just in the hope that the company being sued will settle before trial. It's called legal extortion. If you fail to respond or show up in court the plaintiff gets a default judgment (meaning you lost a phony lawsuit because you didn't show up to contest it in court). In order to sue you, whoever files the lawsuit must first know how who and where to serve you. Guess what? All they have to do today is to enter your name in the Secretary of State database or Google and if your company is registered as part of your corporate structure, they will find your information and resident agent.

Or let's say you lost a personal lawsuit, and you now have an outstanding civil judgment or a tax lien from previous investment activity. It might be perilous to use a publically registered business structure for you to start a new business and to get back on your feet. In extreme cases, a court could "reverse veil pierce" your registered organization. All because you didn't have a privacy curtain to protect your corporate information.

All of this is possible because registering a corporation with the state government leaves a breadcrumb trail that can lead straight back to you and to your business. And since we live in the golden age of surveillance because of the internet, registering a business with the Secretary of State has now become actually dangerous. Even worse, most lawyers don't tell you about the risk inherent in having little privacy for business purposes. They prefer the opposite, transparency, to identify asset targets.

"But that's a very remote risk," some may say. Perhaps. Maybe 99 percent of the time life is good and risk-free. But the remaining one percent is a veritable missile that can utterly destroy you financially. A single hit of that one percent missile and you're screwed. Are you willing to take the risk of not having any type of protection *at all* against a one percent chance of a missile strike to your finances? Can you say with 100 percent certainty that the one percent hit will never happen to you? If you can, then stop reading this book right now because this book is not for you. But if you are less than 100 percent certain, then by all means keep on reading, because what we will see in the next chapters of this book can save you from utter financial destruction.

CHAPTER 3

WHAT IS A BUSINESS TRUST

The Business Trust

A business trust is a commercial business structure based on a private contract among several participants that organizes the ownership and benefits of its assets. Its purpose is to make a profit. It is fundamentally different than a living trust whose purpose is to preserve assets. In essence, multiple participants first agree to create a business, and then decide based upon various practical reasons to use a trust format.

Title and Situs

Before we go any further there are two concepts you must understand in order to protect your business assets. These concepts are 'title' and 'situs.' Title is the legal ownership or an asset. To hold title means to legally own something: Your business, your home, your car, your land, your brokerage accounts, etc. Title is what the official record shows as the owner.

In the case of traditional business structures, shareholders or stockholders own the corporation or LLC which holds legal title. The business trust is set up differently. The legal owner of the assets of the business trust, a trustee, does not necessarily receive the benefits or profits. The beneficiaries do even though they do not own the assets. We will talk about this in detail later in the book.

Situs is the place to which, for purposes of legal jurisdiction or taxation, a property or business belongs. This can be a state or a country. For example, the owner of a company or real property holds title. And the company or real property has situs in a specific state in the United States. So at least in the United States, situs refers primarily to the state in which a property is located or domiciled. In this case, the property could be a corporation itself, or a business trust, and the assets owned by the corporation, LLC or business trust. This is important to understand because the situs of a business itself can be different from the situs for the business's assets. The business can be set up in one state and the assets owned by that business can be in another state.

Traditional business structures, such as corporations or LLCs, have *visible* title because the information about the ownership of the traditional corporation is available to anyone searching public databases. A traditional corporation also has a specific situs, which is the state in which it's domiciled. If you want your company to operate in another state, you have to "naturalize" it, which means you have to register the corporation in that other state.

Business Trusts can easily change situs without naturalization for two reasons: One is because so few states require registration. Second, because the situs of the trust is often based upon the trustees domicile, so a new trustee in another state can quickly move situs.

As we saw in the previous chapter, the way traditional corporations and LLC are setup can be very risky to your privacy and to your wealth. Fortunately, there is a better way to do business with *invisible* title and portable situs to protect your privacy and your property.

Statutory vs. Common Law

Business Trusts are known as *commercial* trusts. There are two types; statutory business trusts and common law business trusts.

Statutory business trusts are relatively new and registered with the state government in a similar way as a traditional business structure. They exist in a handful of states. The primary reason for existence is standardized rules designed for public finance transactions. Mutual funds, for example, often fall under the statutory business trust category. As public companies they have to be registered with the government for investor safety. Examples include the "DST," or Delaware Statutory Trust. Yet statutory business trusts can have many of the same handicaps as corporations and LLCs, a lack of a privacy curtain and exposure to personal information.

Common law business trusts, on the other hand, are generally exempt from registered with the government. They are the original creation. As a result, this type of business trust can offers a privacy curtain and protections unavailable to statutory business trusts and traditional corporate structures. In this book we are focusing on the use of common law business trusts as an instrument to get privacy and liability protections for your assets.

Business trusts are part of a variety of trusts known as commercial trusts. They are also called Massachusetts Business Trusts. 90 percent of trust wealth in the United States is held in commercial trusts which are "business transactions." These business transactions are created by a contract. It is a contractual agreement to do business that establishes who will administer the business and who will benefit from it. We will see this in more detail later.

Unlike traditional corporations or LLCs, business trusts rarely register with the Secretary of State in most states. Business trusts don't have to pay fees, franchise taxes, and they can be set up in a matter of hours.

As a result, unlisted business trusts are completely

invisible to the public because they can't be found in any public database. They're hidden in plain sight. The contract to create a business trust is kept private among the parties involved and given our constitutional rights "to freely contract" it operates without government intrusion. Anyone trying to find out your business information would end up puzzled and frustrated. Think about it as having an unlisted phone number. A business trust is like having an unlisted business. You can use it and it's perfectly legal, but people can't find it. Or like a one-way mirror. You can look outside, but people outside cannot see inside. Your organizational and personal details are safely hidden.

Not only that, but also a business trust can be designed to have simple attributes that you're looking for in your business, instead of conforming to the detailed requirements of the traditional corporate structure.

WHAT IS A BUSINESS TRUST

CHAPTER 4

BANKING AND TAXES WITH A BUSINESS TRUST

Stealth Banking with a Business Trust

Regardless of whether you use a traditional corporation or a business trust for doing business, never mix personal funds with your business funds because in case of a lawsuit or tax audit you are at risk. A traditional corporation or LLC will allow you to open a business bank account so in case of litigation the business's account is on the hook and not your personal account as long as the corporate veil is maintained. But registering a traditional corporation is burdensome and expensive. Fortunately, you can also open a business bank account with a business trust.

Business trusts allow you the flexibility to do business banking with banks that offer accounts for business trusts. When you create a business trust you can get an Employee

Identification Number (EIN) with the Internal Revenue Service (IRS) and then use that EIN to open a business banking account. Unlike a traditional corporation, all of this can be set up in a matter of hours or a couple of business days with minimal paperwork. With a traditional corporation or LLC a bank will ask for a "certificate of good standing" from the Secretary of State in order to allow you to open a business bank account. The "certificate of good standing," which is a certification from the government that you are complying with all of the rules and regulations of a traditional corporation, can take weeks or a month to obtain, delaying you from opening a bank account specifically for business purposes. With a business trust all you need is the EIN in order to open the account. And you can get that done in two to three days instead of several weeks to a month with a traditional corporation.

Even better; when you open a business trust banking account, the account's information is stealthy. And since the business trust itself is not registered with the Secretary of State, nobody will know it even exists. Nobody will be able to look up the information on the account. The bank will require that the trustees (we'll talk about trustees later in the book) as signatories provide photo ID and their social security number, but the account itself does not index the personal information of the trustee. It only indexes the anonymous trust name and EIN, which remains private. As a result, the business trust banking account becomes a stealth banking account. Business trusts also have two options for banking: commercial banking in at institutions like Wells Fargo or Bank of America, or brokerage firms such as Merrill Lynch or Scottrade. There are multiple strategies to choose which type of account to use for a business trust, but several options are available depending on the needs of the trust. You get a stealth bank account using a business trust.

The business trust gives you not just invisibility because of its privacy curtain, but also flexibility, freedom from state governments, speed and savings. That's right; savings. Remember the annual fees and taxes you have to pay for registering a corporation in California? None of those fees and taxes apply to business trusts.

Savings with Business Trusts: No Franchise Taxes and no State Fees

Earlier we saw how you have to pay a minimum of $1,050 fees plus $750 setup costs in order to set up a business in California, and how the $800 California franchise tax means a cost of $4,000 over five years, which can be a lot of money for a small business owner. But since business trusts in California do not have to pay franchise taxes, they pay zero Dollars over those same five years. That's at least $4,000 in savings or more, since the franchise tax is whichever is greater; $800 (minimum) or

8.8% of the income from the business.

In 49 states business trusts are legal. That means, in most states business trusts are not required to be registered with the government. Only in a handful of states statutory business trusts are required to be registered. This means in most states, business trusts are exempt from paying franchise taxes, because they only apply to statutory entities like corporations, LLCs, or Statutory business trusts. Plus, with a business trust you don't have to pay the filing fees associated with registering a traditional corporation or LLC with the Secretary of State.

Just to give you an idea of how much money you can save over the curse of five years by setting up a business trust do the following math on the fees and taxes paid for registering a traditional corporation or LLC:

$800 franchise tax + $100 Secretary of State registration + $150 Resident Agent fee = $1,050 per year. Times 5 years = $5,250 in taxes and fees minimum in order to do business in California.

FEES & TAXES OVER 5 YEARS	
Corporation/LLC	$1,050 x 5 = **$5,250**
Business Trust	$0 x 5 = **$0**

Table 1: Comparison of fees and taxes paid in California in 5 years with a traditional corporation or LLC and with a Business Trust as of 2018. Figures in US Dollars.

But if you use a business trust instead of a traditional corporation or LLC, you pay the following:

$0 franchise tax + $0 Secretary of State registration (since you don't have to register at all) + $0 Resident agent (since you need none) = $0 per year. Times 5 years = $0 in taxes and fees in order to do business in California.

FEES & TAXES	INC/LLC	BT
Secretary of State	$100	$0
Resident Agent	$150	$0
Franchise Tax	**$800**	**$0**
Total	$1,050	$0

Table 2: Comparison of fees and taxes paid in one year in California with a traditional corporation or LLC and with a Business Trust as of 2018. Figures in US Dollars.

There's more. Since you don't have to register a business trust in most states, you can start doing business in different states without having to go through the Secretary of State naturalization process, thus saving even more money. Remember the $5,250 in fees and taxes paid over five years with a traditional corporation in California? If you want to do business in more than one state, you incur more fees and taxes from additional states. But with a business trust you could pay nothing.

And there's even more. What if you wanted to have more than one business? Say, one for selling food and one for selling electronics. If you are in California you would need to file paperwork twice, pay fees and taxes for the first and second business. You'd pay the $1,050 annually for each new INC/LLC you register with the Secretary of State. And that's assuming you're doing the paperwork yourself. If you hire a lawyer to create the package of documents and register them for you, then you could easily pay $750 extra for the legal fees. That's a total of $1,800 for a first time business registration. But if you were to use a business trust, you would not have to register anything nor pay fees and taxes for any of your businesses operated as business trusts. Your franchise taxes and fees would be equal to the amount of business trusts you have times zero. In other words, zero Dollars.

With a business trust, instead of having to do the traditional Secretary of State registration, all you would have to is to fill out the forms for the business trust number two, change the name, change the relevant information for your new business, print the document, and you're ready to go.

By the way; you can have as many business trusts as you want and nobody will be able to find their information in California because guess what? There is no database of business trusts in California. For that matter, there is no database for unlisted business trusts anywhere. Your privacy would be protected and you would save money and time to focus on business operations.

THE *UN*CORPORATION

Three Tax Classifications for Business Trusts

Here's a really important benefit from using a business trust. What about income taxes? For the traditional corporation you just get one classification filed on form 1120. Another problem is if you lose the corporate veil, the tax classification for your business could be lost and you personally could be taxed at individual income tax rates, which are much higher. You could end up owing more taxes plus interest and penalties because you lost the corporate veil in a traditional corporate structure. I wonder when the IRS and FTB will begin to enforce this easy win?

Business Trusts are NOT classified as trusts (1041) for the IRS because they are not simply asset preservation. They are an organization (uncorporation) designed to carry on a business and divide its gains. You get three tax classifications using a trust format.

TAX CLASSIFICATIONS FOR BUSINESS TRUST

BENEFICIARY*	DEFAULT	OPTIONAL**
ONE	DISREGARDED	CORPORATION
TWO OR MORE	PARTNERSHIP	CORPORATION

* Natural Person, INC, LLC or another Trust.
** File form 8832.
Table 3: Comparison of tax classifications for a business trust based upon Treasury Regulations 301.7701-4(b).

In the past business trusts were only taxed as corporations, but in 1997 the Kintner rules changed and business trusts now have three options for tax classification. A business trust is by default taxed as a pass through to the beneficiary-ies. It can optionally elect to be taxed as a corporation by filing form 8832.

(Comment on the side: Some people like the S corporations so they get that passed through back to the personal tax returns to avoid double taxation. But you need to know this; You have a complete loss of privacy on your tax return with the S corporation compared to the C. It may or may not be important to you but just be aware of that fact because now your corporation and your personal tax return are connected together. With the C they're not.)

How a business trust is taxed by default relates to the number of beneficiaries (we will talk about the concept of the beneficiaries in detail in the next chapter). For instance, if your business trust has just one beneficiary you are taxed as an individual. If you have two or more beneficiaries, you are taxed as a partnership. A corporation classification is optional for any number of beneficiaries and can be ideal. In summary, you will need to sort it out with your accountant.

Still, in California and other states business trusts are exempt from paying the state franchise tax. Yet they do have to pay income taxes.

In short, with a traditional corporation you only have

one tax classification. If the corporate veil is pierced during audit, and the owners of the corporation lose the legal protections from the corporate veil, the income from the corporation is recast as personal income and the owners end up owing higher taxes as a result. But with a business trust there is little risk of corporate veil piercing, and thus much safer. With a business trust you get three tax classifications.

Impact of the 2018 Tax Reform

The 2018 Tax Cuts and Jobs Act introduced changes to Federal law that effect business trusts that elect to be taxed as corporations after filing form 8832 with the IRS. In other words, the changes are relevant to any business trust taxed as a corporation. The changes include:

- Corporate tax rate reduced from 35 percent to flat 21 percent.
- Section 12001 repeals corporate Alternative Minimum Tax (AMT) from 20% to zero.
- Section 13543 makes it easier to convert S corporations to C corporations. This creates a benefit for shareholders because dividends distributed during the transition period after the conversion from S to C pay zero taxes.
- Corporations only distribute dividends...but a trust

can also distribute capital gains.

- There are accommodations for controlled foreign corporations, sourced income, cash holdings and foreign tax credits.

Again, these changes and benefits are relevant to business trusts that file 'check the box' on IRS form 8832 to be taxed as a corporation. You must submit form 8832 to get corporate classification. Failure to do so can have punitive consequences for the beneficiaries as you will be taxed at the default classification.

CHAPTER 5

MORE BENEFITS OF A BUSINESS TRUST

The Benefits of Invisibility

I can't underscore this enough. The invisibility of a business trust's privacy curtain can provide you a form of insurance against lawsuits and other business risks. There's no way to look up the information about the business trust itself. Imagine the name of your new business trust. Try typing the name of a company set up as a business trust on Google and you're not going to find it. This means if anyone wants to sue you it will be very difficult (compared to corporations or LLCs) for them to do it, since they won't be able to find your business information, and therefore they won't know who to sue or where to file the lawsuit. If you have told others about your business trust some attorneys may be able to do the research on who and where to sue (and even so it will be difficult to find the information), but most garden variety lawyers don't even know where to start. On the other hand, with a traditional corporation an attorney can simply look up the corporate registration on a website and use that information to build a lawsuit against your company.

By the way; traditional corporations are easy to sue *by design*. Remember you have to file a Resident Agent with the Secretary of State for a traditional corporation or LLC? The purpose to the Resident Agent is to receive legal notices for the company. Which means if somebody wants to sue the company, it couldn't be easier. Is really your job to make it easier for the world to sue you? Your business and property is safer if you are tough target. Be the green fruit in the top of a tree. Be elusive and difficult. There's no resident agent for a business trust.

What if you are a high profile personality in business, in sports, in politics, in entertainment, or in the media? What if your name is immediately recognizable? A lot of scary people could be looking up your name and find property, businesses, and other assets. So by using a business trust for your business and assets you get a privacy curtain. Anonymity feels safer. It gives you protection from business data hackers, identity theft, from nosy people, gossips, and from people wanting to sue or hurt you just to see if they can get away with it.

That means a business trust could be considered as a

form of insurance for you and your property. Remember; perhaps life is good and safe 99 percent of the time. But if you happen to get hit with the one percent of the times that life is not good and safe, what will protect you from financial destruction? Well, a business trust could provide you with some form of insurance against that one percent risk. We buy insurance to have peace of mind in the event of an emergency. For example, fire insurance, life insurance, earthquake insurance, health insurance, car insurance. Ask yourself the following: How much is peace of mind worth to you? It's invaluable. A privacy curtain is priceless because it saves you time by eliminating worry. The best part is, this form of insurance, the business trust, has a relatively nominal cost to set up.

State Portable

This is why the business trust is not just invisible, but also flexible and portable. Your unlisted business trust can be used to do business in most any state where there's no requirement for registration. Your business can cross state lines with ease and without having to "naturalize" it (as do INC/LLCs) in another state. Furthermore, simply moving your trustee to another state or selecting a trustee in another state affords the business trust great portability.

Insurance Against Corporate Identity Theft

"Wait. Did you say corporate identity theft? That actually exists?" some may ask. Oh yes. It does exist.

Business identity theft happens when somebody obtains your corporation or LLC information, forges documentation to make them look like they are your corporate documents and then engages in fraudulent transactions using your business information. If somebody steals your corporate identity and engages in fraudulent transactions, your business could be entangled in litigation or at the very least in intrusive investigations while things clear up. At a minimum, this will dilute your business focus from what it's supposed to do: make money for you. At worst, it could mean you losing money or facing distraction because of litigation or complications related to the investigation in the corporate theft.

But with a business trust you're safe because nobody can find your information online. If nobody can find your business information, nobody can steal your business identity, thus giving you once again a form of insurance against this type of contingency.

No Corporate Veil Risk

Here's another benefit from having a business trust instead of a traditional corporation: minimal risk of having the corporate veil pierced. Remember how the corporate veil can be jeopardized if you fail to comply with all of the government red tape and regulations for traditional business structures? Remember how your business contracts can be voided if the corporate veil is lifted and how YOU can be held responsible personally if your company gets sued? You might also be personally responsible for debts of the corporation. Well, few of those risks exist with the business trust. Since federal and state governments do not regulate our constitutional right to freely contract, those state governments can't jeopardize your business trust. Furthermore, there are few if any authorities with expertise or charged with overseeing business trusts. Your contracts would be safe, your minimal recordkeeping, and your property would not be easy targets to challenge.

Business Restart Insurance

One more benefit from having a business trust. Let's say something does happen and your corporation gets hit with a civil judgment or a tax lien. Or you got a personal civil judgment or tax lien for other reason unrelated to your business. If that were to happen with a traditional business structure, the civil judgment and the tax liens could attach to you personally and to your property if the corporate veil is pierced. Regardless of how you got the judgment or tax liens, those obligations are listed in the general index of the county where you reside, until satisfied. And if you have any personal assets such as real estate, and you need to sell a piece for capital to start a new business and get back on your feet, the money from the sale could be swept away in escrow in order to pay for the tax lien or judgment.

With a business trust, if your business gets hit with financial or legal trouble you would be isolated personally from a civil judgment or tax lien because of the structure of the business trust. (we will see why in more detail later in the book.) And if you get a civil judgment or tax lien personally for another reason, a business trust can help you to restart a new business because it is unlisted and legally isolated from you personally.

So by having a business trust you can have the means to get back on your feet and start a new business quietly and with a lot less stress and restrictions. If unforeseen trouble happens, as it always does along the way for successful business people, you should have the opportunity to get back on your feet and start over. With a traditional business structure there are multiple risks to address. With a business trust, getting back on your feet is much safer and easier.

Benefits on the Cost of Litigation

In a lawsuit against a traditional corporation or LLC, an

attorney may offer your opponent, the plaintiff, a contingency fee plan because there is a clear legal roadmap to identify corporate assets. A contingency fee happens when instead of asking for a legal fee or a retainer up front, an attorney offers to work for a percent of the economic award given to the plaintiff in a judgment if the plaintiff wins the case. This can happen if the attorney knows how much money or assets the accused, your corporation, has and if the attorney calculates the case can be easy to win. Because attorneys can easily find bank account balances and assets of a traditional corporation or LLC, and thus calculate how much money the accused corporation or LLC is worth (liquid cash to get paid), they may conclude a contingency fee is more profitable for the attorney than an upfront fee. This no cash upfront option makes it easy for their client to proceed with a lawsuit against you. As a result, traditional corporations and LLCs offer attorneys an incentive to go after them, and to get as much of your money as possible.

In contrast, the bank accounts and assets as well as situs of an unlisted business trust are difficult for the attorney to discover. As a result, the attorney is highly unlikely to offer a contingency fee and, instead, charge a $10,000 retainer fee upfront, which could dissuade less than seriously determined and financed plaintiffs from suing. Plaintiff may think twice about suing if the attorney demands money up front for an open ended rabbit hunt.

With a contingency fee, a plaintiff has an easier ride to sue. With an upfront retainer, the plaintiff needs an open and fat checkbook.

In other words, corporate lawyers and attorneys know corporations are easy to sue and, as a result, they have an economic incentive to sue a traditional corporation or LLC. Just read the financial news. Whether you like it or not, it's called legal extortion. But with unlisted business trusts, important details are fuzzy by design. There is no clear roadmap. As a result, clients will pay dearly upfront and monthly for their attorneys to hunt and learn how and where to pursue a business trust.

Minimal Paperwork

Earlier we saw how with traditional corporations you have to fill out and keep records of several types of paperwork, from the registration forms, to director and shareholder meeting minutes and resolutions. And these obligations must happen every year to maintain the corporate veil. But with a business trust the paperwork is minimal. You simply generate the business trust declaration among the parties who participate in the trust, sign it, notarize it, get the EIN from the IRS, open the business bank account, and you're set to go.

You do have to keep some common sense records as a prudent policy, such as change of trustee, bank records and a beneficiary list (we'll talk about trustees and beneficiaries in more detail later) but the amount of paperwork you're required to do with a corporation or LLC is huge compared to what you need to do with a business trust. So if you don't like paperwork which can jeopardize the corporate veil, this is another reason to earnestly consider a business trust.

No Name Conflicts

And one more benefit from the business trust for your business: you can pick pretty much any name you want for your business. If you were to register a corporation with the Secretary of State, you would need to research the registration database to see if the name is available or already taken. If it is, you can't use it. But with a business trust you can use almost any name. However, you do need to put some thought to the name you are going to pick. What image to convey? In order to protect your privacy you want a name that's not going to identify you personally. But since you can use almost any name for a business trust, creating a name should be easy, as there will not be any conflicts with the names already registered with the Secretary of State. After all, the Secretary of State rules don't apply to your business trust.

This also applies when you move your business to another state. Let's say you have a traditional corporation in California named ABC Business. You've invested heavily in marketing the name brand. But now you want to start doing business in Colorado. You're in the process of registering your business in Colorado but you bump into a problem: somebody else in Colorado already registered the name ABC Business. This means you're blocked from use your own name in a different state. But with a business trust you don't have to worry about inter-state name conflicts because there are very few registries for business trusts. Advertising is a different issue. As a result, you can use your business name almost anywhere without having the problem of a name conflict.

Potential Handicaps and Solutions

In case you're wondering, there are some potential handicaps in using a business trust. They are minimal, but you should be aware of them.

Handicap 1: Lawyers. When you want to use a business trust and you need to hire a lawyer to handle the business legal issues, you will need a lawyer who is skilled in business law, contracts and commercial trusts. At its core, a business trust is a contract among the parties who participate in it, so you will need a lawyer who understands contracts to handle the legal issues successfully. You're not looking for a lawyer who advertises living trusts, family law, or a generic, garden variety lawyer. You are looking for a specific type of lawyer who specializes in contracts, business law and commercial trusts. Be aware that a living trust lawyer's focus is estate planning. This is a different expertise. You are looking for a specific type of lawyer who specializes in contracts, business law and commercial trusts.

Handicap 2: Accountants. The accountant for your business trust should be aware of Treasury Regulations 301.7701. The entire regulations are relevant, but 301.7701-4(b) refers specifically to business trust taxation.

Handicap 3: Financial Institutions. You can only open a business account with a bank that offers accounts for business trusts or unincorporated associations. Not all banks offer them, but many do, including some of the biggest banks in the country. You will need to find out which banks offer business trust accounts. And this takes a little research, because if you walk to the front desk at the bank, chances are the receptionist is not going to know if the bank offers accounts for business trusts. So you will need to do some digging in order to find a bank for your business trust. This search is easiest done online. You will find that Brokerage firms are more sophisticated with trust accounts.

Handicap 4: DBA Statement. If you want to do business with the public you may need to file a DBA statement. DBA stands for "Doing Business As." In other words, it's the fictitious name you pick for the front door sign of your business, not the name your business is actually registered as officially. The statement would say that "ABC Business Trust is doing business as XYZ Investment Management Company." The business trust would not be listed in with the Secretary of State, but it would be listed with the county or city's DBA statement. The good thing is, if somebody looks up the business name and they find your business trust, they're not going to be able to find additional information from the Secretary of State.

As you can see, these handicaps are quite small when you compare them to the overall business trust benefits.

Why do You Want a Business Trust

Time again to ask yourself if you want a business trust. The answer is NO if you:

•Have a team of lawyers on speed dial and the money to pay for them.
•Dismiss the significance of asset privacy.
•Feel immune to life's financial surprises.
•Don't believe a business privacy curtain is critical in today's tech security world.
•Are OK with paying franchise taxes.

The answer is YES if you want to:

•Keep nosy people and hackers out of your

financial affairs.

•Be a tough target for opportunists and plaintiff lawyers.

•Feel safer with a privacy curtain.

•Have your assets and bank accounts off public radar screens.

•Less paperwork requirements.

•Legal advantages a traditional corporation won't give you.

•Do business across state lines easily.

•Taxation flexibility.

If your answer is yes, then keep on reading because in the next chapter we will look into detail at the actual components that make up a business trust. Understanding these components will allow you to implement the privacy curtain and property protections available in a business trust to the fullest.

MORE BENEFITS OF A BUSINESS TRUST

CHAPTER 6

THE COMPONENTS OF A BUSINESS TRUST

Now that we know about the benefits of a business trust, let's take a look under the hood in order to understand how it works. Generally, a for profit business trust has three primary participants: a trustor, a trustee or trustees, and beneficiaries.

The Trustor

The trustor, also known as the grantor, is the person or legal entity that initiates the trust by arranging to have his property put under the management of one or more trustees for the benefit of one or more beneficiaries. In other words, the trustor is the person who wants some form of property assets to be enhanced by somebody (the trustee) to make a profit for the benefit of somebody else (the beneficiaries.) In many cases beneficiaries are the grantor. To put it another way, the trustor is giving his property (nominal or significant) to somebody for the benefit of somebody else.

The Trustee

The trustee is the legal owner of the business trust. In other words, the trustee holds the title to trust assets. However, the fact that the trustee owns the trust doesn't mean s/he will get the benefits from the trust. The trustee is in essence a director of the trust who oversees the trust and can earn a fee for being a trustee. But the real benefits from the trust do not go to the trustee. They go to the beneficiaries. Trustees also have liability safety because they act in a fiduciary capacity on behalf of the beneficiaries. Trustees can earn trustee's fees. Trustees can be a corporation or individual(s).

The Beneficiaries

The beneficiaries can be one or more persons who will receive the profits from the trust without being the legal owners. They can also be a grantor of the trust. The trustees determine and distribute the amount of benefits, typically money, the beneficiaries will get. So while the trustee is the legal owner of the trust, the beneficiaries are the ones who actually profit from it. Beneficiaries can also be thought of as stockholders from a corporation or shareholder members from an LLC. But in a corporation the stockholders are legal owners. In an LLC shareholder members are legal owners. In a business trust beneficiaries are *not* legal owners, the trustees are.

This is an important distinction to make because the legal owners in a corporation or LLC might be sued personally precisely because they are the legal owners. If they get sued personally for any reason such as automobile accident or in a divorce, their stock or member shares are now at risk, or attachable because these assets are part of their personal property estate. In a business trust beneficiaries are not legal owners and, as a result, they don't have the same attachment risk as in traditional business structures. Thus, beneficiaries have limited liability safety from both business and personal events.

Bifurcation

This trustee and beneficiary structure has one important distinction for all parties involved: *Bifurcation,* which means splitting a main body into two components. Bifurcation is unique to the business trust and not found in traditional corporations or LLCs. In a business trust, bifurcation means that the business structure is separated into two components, the legal owner and the beneficial owner. The trustees get title, while beneficiaries get the money.

What the trustee does is independent from what the beneficiaries do. Trustee and beneficiary are isolated from one another. There is no agency relationship between trustee and beneficiaries.

Agency refers to the legal relationship between a principal and its representative agent. An agent acts on behalf of somebody else and the agent's actions have legal status as a representative of the principal. A real estate agent, for example, has the legal authority to sell a house owned by and on behalf of a client because the agent is representing the owner of the house. Other examples of agency include corporate officers acting on behalf of stockholders, or a power of attorney you give someone.

In a trust, there is no agency between trustees and beneficiaries because a trust agreement does not give trustees representation over beneficiaries. Trustees only have managing control over assets owned by the trust, not the beneficiaries.

This means the actions of the trustee will not affect the beneficiaries and vice versa. The trustee has no legal responsibility as a consequence of the personal actions of the beneficiaries. And the beneficiaries do not have any obligations as a consequence of the personal actions of the trustee. The trustee can't have legal responsibility over the actions of the beneficiaries because the trustee is only operating as a fiduciary, not as an agent. And the beneficiaries don't have legal responsibility over the actions of the trustee, and the trust, for that matter, because legally they are not the owners of the trust. They only enjoy the financial benefits of the trust.

BIFURCATION	TRUSTEE	BENEFICIARY
LEGAL OWNER	YES	NO
ASSET CONTROL	YES	NO
CONTRACT FOR ASSETS	YES	NO
PROFITS	NO	YES
OVERVIEW	TRUSTEE	BENEFICIARY
ATTORNEY IN FACT	NO	NO
AGENCY	NO	NO
FIDUCIARY DUTY	YES	NO

Table 4: Illustration of Trustee and Beneficiary.

To better understand consider the following: Let's say a trust is created to run a business. The trustee will get a fee for managing the trust and the beneficiaries will get the actual profits from the business. One day one of the beneficiaries gets sued personally and the plaintiff wants to get compensation from the beneficiary's assets. Well, the plaintiff's lawyers won't be able to touch the trust assets because the beneficiary is not an owner. And since the actual legal owner, which is the trustee, is not involved in the lawsuit, the financial benefits from the trust for the beneficiary remain legally protected.

The opposite is also true. What if somebody sues the trustee personally? If that were to happen the beneficiaries would not be a party to that lawsuit because they don't legally own the trust. And since the trustees are only acting as appointed fiduciaries, trust assets are safe. This is because trust assets are not the trustees' personal assets.

As a result, bifurcation makes a trust unique and difficult target for lawsuits, thus providing legal protections for beneficiaries and trustees unlike traditional corporate structures.

Remember, in a traditional corporation or LLC when the veil is lifted, the stockholders or shareholder members as legal owners can be personally liable. With a business trust there is no corporate veil and suing the beneficiaries will not yield trust assets. One more thing: if a beneficiary gets sued, the other beneficiaries are unaffected because, again, they are not co-owners. The activities of one beneficiary are independent from the others. The trust provides benefits, but no responsibilities or agency relationship exist between one another.

The bifurcation structure has another advantage over

traditional corporate structures. Upon death of a trustee or beneficiary, the trust continues to operate without interruption. Trustees are replaced, beneficiaries are replaced. In a traditional corporation or LLC, if a majority stockholder or a shareholder dies, and their estate is probated, it could freeze business operations and all banking into a standstill.

In conclusion, as a result of bifurcation, business trusts have greater flexibility and safety mechanisms than traditional corporations.

Financial Identity

You may be wondering "wait a minute, if the trustee is the asset owner and the beneficiaries only get benefits, then how does the business trust get financial identity for doing business?" Well, through the trust's Employee Identification Number or EIN. The EIN is the trust's fiscal identity issued by the IRS. Neither the trustee nor the beneficiaries will use their personal information for the operation of the trust. Once again, personal privacy is protected.

The EIN, by the way, is used in a business trust for banking, brokerage firms and for investments. As we saw in the previous chapter, the bank account created with the business trust's EIN is virtually a stealth bank account, since no personal names, social security numbers or other personal information is indexed with the bank account. Although the trustee signatories are known to the bank, only the Trust EIN and name is indexed with the business accounts.

CHAPTER 7

WHAT CAN I DO WITH A BUSINESS TRUST

B usiness trusts can be used for a variety of purposes. They are particularly powerful tools for risk reduction, anonymous transactions, and privacy. Here is a brief list of actual real life uses that are very difficult to achieve with a corporation or LLC, but that are available with a business trust.

Risk Reduction:

- Avoid Pre-Nuptial Contracts
- Isolate Dangerous or Hazardous Equipment/Operations
- Safeguard Personal Assets from the Business
- Avoid Secretary of State & Resident Agent

WHAT CAN I DO WITH A BUSINESS TRUST

- Alternative or Complement to Asset Protection
- Asset Divestiture — Legal Owner to Beneficiary
- Quickly Transfer Assets to any Jurisdiction
- Divide Marital Property
- Assets in Low Tax State
- Safer than Open Account of Dissolved Entity
- Onshore Alternative to Offshore
- Neutralize Investor Lawsuits
- Diversify Ownership of Portfolio

Anonymous Transactions:

- Investing
- Precious Stones & Gold
- Hedge Funds
- Managed Futures
- Private Equity
- Private Placements
- Forex
- Business Sale
- Outside Estate Plan — Direct to Successor

Privacy:

- Automobile Collections
- Art Collections
- Bank Accounts

- Brokerage Accounts
- Unlisted New Business
- Bearer LLC Shareholder
- Bearer INC Stockholder
- Foreign Nationals

And there's more. Business trusts are part of three main types of trusts that are available for different purposes, including holding title to real estate and other forms of asset protection. That is the subject if the next chapter.

WHAT CAN I DO WITH A BUSINESS TRUST

CHAPTER 8

WHAT TYPES OF TRUST ARE THERE

To better understand why a business trust is an invaluable business arrangement model, let's take a quick look at the history and types of trusts that have existed for centuries.

There are several types of trusts. Each type of trust is unique because it has a different purpose. Most people have heard about living (personal) as well as charitable trusts, which are set up to manage how legacies, money or assets are going to be given to others as gifts after death. There are also real property (realty) trusts, informally called land trusts specifically designed to manage and own real estate (not REIT). The third type which we've been talking about in this book is the business (commercial) trust. That is, a for profit enterprise organized in a trust format.

Personal Trust

Personal estate trusts date back to the times of the early Romans. The Roman called it *fideicommissa* (or *fideicommissum* in the plural), a Latin word, which literally means to commit trust. Fideicommissa was an economic tool used by elite Romans citizens to evade civil laws and arrange for a legacy or the inheritance of property. For example, a rich property owner would designate a citizen heir as trustee without actually naming his daughter beneficiary because of Lex Voconia, a breach of rules on capacity. As a result, instructions to the trustee to convey the property to the beneficiary (sui heredes) were verbal and moral obligations. Fideicommissa meant 'immortality' for the testator.

In the German Civil Code of Private Law our trust instrument is called *Treuhand*.

Today, personal trusts are often known as living (inter-vivos) trusts. They have evolved and changed significantly over the centuries. Trust funds, for example, are personal trusts in which a trustor designates a trustee to manage money and assets for beneficiaries. However, personal trusts are not designed to conduct business, but to preserve and manage gifts such as inheritances, insurance, legacies and charities.

THE *UN*CORPORATION

Real Property Trust

Realty trust law emerged in England during the Middle Ages, specifically during the 12th and 13th centuries, at the time of the Crusades and under the feudal system.

In one example at that time, when a Knight landowner (feoffor) left England to fight in the Crusades, he designated the ownership of his land during his absence to a manager (feoffee) who would manage the property, pay and receive feudal dues, but with the promise and understanding that the property ownership would be returned to its original owner upon return from the Crusades.

The problem was, at that time English common law only recognized legal title, not this type of equity arrangement. When the designated manager refused to return the ownership of the land to the Knight, this Crusader would have to petition directly to the King, who would turn the case to his Lord Chancellor, who could decide the case in favor of the Crusader. It is from this practice (substance over form) that equitable jurisdiction evolved, designating the manager as the trustee and the landowner (in this case the Knight) as the true beneficiary.

Additionally, serfs in England had no protection against the Crown, and their property was under constant risk of being seized simply because of a mere accusation of treason, capricious taxes, or refusal of military duty.

As a result, serfs arranged to put the ownership of their land under a trust agreement with a Duke. The agreement would give the Duke the legal ownership of the serf's land and a third of the proceeds from rents and shares of the land's production. In exchange, the Duke would act as a trustee and thus protect the serf's land against the Crown. Serfs would become beneficiaries from the agreement and get 70 percent of the proceeds from the land, as well as peace of mind by knowing their lands would be protected.

Serfs made this type of arrangement with the Dukes because in the English Magna Carta, signed by King John in 1215, the King became subservient to the nobility. Therefore, as long as the Dukes had enough political power over the Crown, the Crown would not be able to touch their property, making the Dukes a perfect trustee for serf land.

Monasteries of Franciscan Friars also had challenges with the 'Statutes of Mortmain.' Local community leaders became trustees of the Monastery to defeat the feudal system.

During the 15th and 16th centuries, property trusts were a way of avoiding feudal taxes. Back then the law stated that if a person died, the King was entitled to money from the property before the land passed to an heir. If there were no heirs, then all of the property would go to the Crown. Therefore, transferring the title of the property to a group of trustees for common use guaranteed this taxation would never happen. Henry VIII tried to prohibit this type of property trust with the 'Statute of Uses' because it deprived the Crown of revenue. A century later, as the Crown got revenue from mercantile activity, property trusts became more popular and tolerated by the Crown.

By the 18th century the use of trusts in England became formalized. In the arrangement of the property trust, land was to be held by a trustee for the benefit of somebody else. And the Courts of Chancery recognized officially the beneficiary as the true equitable owner of the property. These unique realty trusts also exist in the United States.

Commercial Trust

The business trust is one of the many modern forms of commercial trusts that has been developed since the 18th century not just for holding title to land, but to engage in commercial activities and other economic purposes. Its purpose is to administer private wealth and make a profit for the beneficiaries. Commercial trusts include, among others, Mutual Funds, Secured Finance, Public Agencies, International Companies, the US Social Security Trust Fund, and Pension Plans. Commercial trusts are also used by sophisticated investors in order to have a privacy curtain that can obscure business assets.

TRUST CATEGORIES

PERSONAL (GIFT)	COMMERCIAL (INVESTMENT)
INTER-VIVOS LIVING	SOCIAL SECURITY
CHARITABLE	REAL ESTATE INVESTMENT TRUST (REIT)
FOUNDATIONS	PENSION PLANS
INSURANCE	BUSINESS
ANNUITY	MUTUAL FUNDS

Table 5: Comparison between the personal and commercial trusts.

"Weren't there laws against business trusts? Aren't there antitrust laws?" some may ask. The answer is this: antitrust laws and other efforts to apparently legislate against trusts in reality are not intended against trusts, but against the activities some business trusts were engaging in. For example, Standard Oil was a business trust, but it acted as a monopoly, making John D. Rockefeller the richest man in the history of the world in the late 19th century. The laws were designed to stop monopolies (Sherman Act) and price fixing (Clayton Act), not to prohibit business trusts. They are called antitrust laws because some trusts were engaging in monopolistic behavior and predatory pricing, but the trusts themselves were not the target of legislation. What was being targeted by that legislation was the *behavior* for which business trusts were being used (in this case monopolies), but not the business trusts as legal business structures. They have never been outlawed or deemed illegal. That is why business trusts continue to operate today holding trillions of US Dollars in assets.

Still, many wealthy people use Business trusts as part of their wealth management strategies. Why? Because of the legal and financial protections unlisted commercial trusts offer can't be obtained with a statutory business trust nor with a traditional corporate structure: invisibility, portability, stealth banking, no Secretary of State registration and fees, no franchise taxes, and no legal burdens and risks inherent in traditional corporations and LLCs.

The Purpose of the Trust

As you now know, the basic architecture of a trust includes – grantor, trustee and beneficiary. These three participants exist in all types – personal, real property, and commercial.

You might think you can substitute one trust for another. But there's a difference. Each type has a unique purpose (reason for being) and function (activity). For example...

The purpose of personal trust is for gifting and functions as estate distribution. The purpose of a real property trust is for holding title and functions as an ownership device. The purpose of commercial trust is to make a profit and functions as a business.

You can also think of an LLC replaced by a real estate land trust, and a corporation replaced with a business trust.

But despite the fact that business trusts have existed for a long time, and for some they are a better business structure than traditional corporations, very few people know about them and about their benefits for privacy, portability, and legal liability protections. The knowledge of the use of commercial trusts for privacy and legal safety, which is the precise subject of this book, is a missing scarce resource you can hardly find even on the internet in a concise, easy to understand form. Why? That is the subject of the next chapter.

CHAPTER 9

REACTIVE AND PROACTIVE

There's a good chance at some point in this book you asked yourself the following question: "why haven't I heard of business trusts before?" There are two main reasons. One: Because lawyers and other affected parties simply don't know about them or make money with business trusts. And two: Because of human nature, our reactive mindset. Let's take a look at both of these reasons in more detail.

One: Lawyers and Other Affected Parties go Broke with Business Trusts

Lawyers usually don't know much about business trusts because they're not taught in law school. What they do learn about is personal trusts (also known as living trusts) for inheritance, insurance or charities so they can maybe earn a living. Even business experts often don't know much about business trusts or how to use them because business schools rarely mention them except in a passing historical context. They may know about trust funds and other types of trusts that are used to manage gifts, but, rarely about the commercial use of trusts for business transactions.

Lawyers are taught 'transparency' and 'full disclosure.' This runs counter to our privacy objective. And even if lawyers did know about unlisted business trusts, they don't have an incentive to tell you about it because then you would need their services less and earn less money. Lawyers charge for corporate filings and record keeping. That's often their bread and butter income. Also, remember how you need to pay for a Resident Agent in order to receive legal notices if you want to register a traditional corporation? Remember how corporate lawyers prefer corporations because they are easy to sue? If you were to use a business trust instead of a traditional corporation, you would not need a whole bunch of busy corporate filings and record keeping, nor a Resident Agent, nor a corporate lawyer. What lawyer wants to earn less money? Traditional corporations and LLCs are good money makers for the legal community.

Our business trusts are lousy money makers for law firms because there's very little paperwork to take care of. If business trusts were good income producers for lawyers, they would be doing it. But they're not because it deprives them of income even though a business trust could mean a lot of benefits for you as their client, a business person. Lawyers can make money with statutory business trusts associated with REITS or big money public finance. But they share many of the secretary of state registration characteristics as traditional corporations and LLCs such as public visibility and resident agents. But not so much in the case of unlisted business trusts, which is the subject of this book.

State government is also not going to tell you about business trusts because they lose filing fees, renewal fees and in many cases franchise taxes if you do not register a traditional corporation. The Secretary of State's office simply don't have an incentive to make information on business trusts available to the public.

As a result, there is scarce financial education on business trusts available to the public. It's missing. There is one solution to this problem, though: knowledge. The more you're informed about business trusts (reading this book, for example), the more options available to you.

Two: Because of the Reactive Mindset

By the very nature of human beings, we're all busy. The majority of people typically don't look for new ways to do business because we are trained to obey, comply and take the default option. We're reactive. In our case, the default option is to register a traditional corporation or LLC without thinking. Yet they expose themselves to tremendous risk by going into business using their personal information. People also learn to follow the rules, so they follow the rules of traditional business structures without asking if there's a different way of doing things.

This habit of picking the default option and follow its rules is what I call the reactive mentality. It's a type of passive approach in which you react to what you are told to do and jump accordingly. It's great for whoever told you (lawyers) to act in a certain way, but it may be completely against your own interests. Again, this is normal. It is how most human beings are by nature. We conform to social rules of the herd.

Reactive mentalities often find the default or "known" option to be safe, even when the default option operates against whoever uses them. You want to do business but you don't know how, so you ask and somebody tells you to register a corporation because that's how most people do it. You think that makes sense and you register the corporation, perhaps thinking whoever told you is acting in your best interest (and perhaps whoever told you to use the default option also thinks he's acting in your best interest), so you feel OK in the knowledge that you did what you were told.

The problem is, as we have seen in this book, if you register a traditional corporation you will be paying a lot of money and expose yourself, your privacy, and your property to unnecessary risk. You passively reacted to what you were told without exploring other possibilities, and you feel safe about your decision but you are in fact placing yourself at risk without knowing it. What you don't know you don't know, until now.

Registering a traditional corporation, instead of using a business trust is therefore part of the reactive mindset. It's the default and understood way to do business, but perhaps not the best for you in our internet era.

The Proactive Mentality

The opposite of the reactive mentality is the proactive mentality, which is an active way of thinking that allows people to explore other options in *advance* of a future situation instead of simply conforming to the default way of doing things.

In our situation, a proactive mentality will look for a different way of doing business that's actually *designed* to that person's needs or objectives yet safe. Instead conforming to the rules that have been pre-baked with traditional business structures, an unlisted business trust is the result of a proactive mentality. We take control of design to fit the needs of the entrepreneur or investor.

The reactive mindset passively obeys and takes whatever business structure is ready made for them, while the proactive mentality will seek to create what that person want as the design for his/her business.

Al humans have reactive minds. But some learn how to think proactively. A proactive mind has to be trained. Independent thinkers who develop a proactive mind resist conformity to default options and find different ways of doing things. It's actually a more efficient and less stressful way to live.

Being that the case, ask yourself the following business question: would you rather conform to the rules somebody else has already made for you even if they don't act in your best interest? If so, the traditional corporation or LLC is perfect for you. Or would you rather create your own design that better fits your needs, providing a privacy curtain and legal protections to you and your business?

Asset Protection or Privacy

Protection is generally a defensive setup of traditional corporations, family limited partnerships or LLCs. They're very expensive and complex to provide a legal fortress in the event of attack. Again, these are reactive by default. Courts and lawyers are like a sticky spider's web. Once trapped, You feel like you'll never get out.

Asset protection schemes are often based in the Cook Islands, Bahamas, Nevada, Alaska, or Delaware. But what these lawyers don't explain is that unless your actual assets themselves (versus the legal owner) have physical situs in that jurisdiction, they're at risk from local courts.

Privacy is an offensive setup of anonymous unlisted business trusts. They're priceless and simple because they help you avoid attack. It is proactive by design. Even if you already have "protection" setup, drape a privacy curtain in front of your assets for double safety.

Protection is preparation for legal battle. Stealth is to avoid legal battle.

REACTIVE AND PROACTIVE

CHAPTER 10

HOW DO I SET UP A BUSINESS TRUST?

Is the Business Trust for You?

At this point in the book you are probably fully aware of the risks of the traditional corporation and the many advantages you can get by *un*corporating using a business trust; privacy protection, money savings, far less paperwork, time savings, stealth banking, state portability, and many more. You're an entrepreneur, a business person, a high profile person, and you want the privacy curtain and legal advantages that come with a business trust. Maybe you have used traditional business structures in the past but you want to try a new direction because now you're realizing it's not necessary to complicate doing business when it doesn't need to be.

HOW DO I SET UP A BUSINESS TRUST

Maybe want to something similar to what Fox News and Wall Street Journal owner Rupert Murdoch did when he divested himself from a television station by using a business trust. By using a business trust, Murdoch did not give up absolute control over the station, but he did give up legal ownership of it, smart. Maybe you want something similar to what the Waltons, the owners of Walmart, did when they used a business trust to hold some of their real estate.

Or maybe you're looking to set up a business for the first time and you realize now that the business trust is the easiest, quickest and safest way to set up your business.

If any of the above is the case, then you're probably wondering how to get your own business trust. If that's the case, then you have two options: you can either get an expert to set up a business trust for you, or you can learn how to do it yourself. It's tough finding someone to do it for you, they're in world financial capitals such as New York or London. But because the knowledge and strategies of unlisted business trusts is rare, the cost is upwards of $25,000 to have it done for you. But if you learn how to do it yourself, you only pay once for the learning experience a fraction of the cost. After that, you can set up as many business trusts as you want with nominal expenses.

What Could You Learn About
Business Trusts?

Let's say you want to learn how to set up a business trust by yourself. Then there are strategies to apply. So you need to know exactly what to look for. Here are some examples:

What will be the name of the business trust? Not all names work the same. And some of them can be risky. Do you use initials? Do you use roman numerals? Why?

How do you pick the trustees for the business trust? Who, where, how many and why will the trustees be? Not picking the right trustees can also be a risk.

And what about beneficiaries? Who and why will the beneficiaries be? Is it an individual? Is it a corporation, LLC or a partnership? Is it a living trust? These are important questions to consider carefully before filling in the blanks on your business trust documents.

What about the EIN? There are some sensitive questions in the IRS SS-4 form for the EIN that you need to be aware of. (you do not need a SSN, EIN or ITIN to get your Business Trust EIN). And what about the assets that will be part of the business trust? Which ones are OK to put into a business trust and which ones are not?

What about the bank account? Where do you get the bank account? Why? And how many bank accounts do you have? Who are the signatories?

"Wait. Aren't there any blank forms online that I can just fill out in order to do a business trust?" some may ask. The answer is not likely. There are virtually no such forms online. And if you were to find them, they would not have any depth to them. This is the hazard with all blank forms. They are incapable of explaining to you important considerations you need to be aware of when you set up a business trust because there's no strategy. Remember: business trusts are not default business structures. They are *designed* for our specific needs, privacy. It is almost an *artisanal* way of setting up a business. A blank form is not going to give you the design for your specific needs, it's flat. It's never going to help you decide how, why, and where because it lacks context. Once you get the basic strategies internalized you can easily get up and going. This is a much more dynamic and effective approach.

Remember how you need to know where to go, where to land, how much fuel you will need and so on in order to fly a plane without incident? That's the flight plan. And you need a flight plan for setting up a business trust if you want to get the maximum benefits and the least risk from it. The amount of money you can save you over time by learning how to do this is tremendous.

The business trust is a unique, powerful tool that you want and need. And they're scarce. Very few people know what it is, how to set it up, or how to use it. Find out for yourself.

Think about is this way: If you learn how to set up your own business trust, and you use that knowledge to actually set one up, in a few months you will look back with a smile, with a relief, knowing you got it done. You're up and going. You got a privacy curtain. You got stealth and peace of mind. You're free from the secretary of state. You are now one of the few who know how to take full advantages of the *un*corporation. You will have an edge over your competition. And you will have that edge for life.

Where can I get more information?

trustarte.com
trustartesolutions.com

Trustarte is the Leading Provider of Asset Privacy Solutions for Banking, Real Estate and Business.

01 619 537-8625 (text/voice)
01 619 425-6500 (fax)

cs@trustarte.com (email)

HOW DO I SET UP A BUSINESS TRUST

EPILOGUE

WHAT LAWYERS WON'T TELL YOU

Just as I was finishing up this book I attended an event about asset protection. This is because I wanted to find out their current strategies. Do they now use business trusts? Had they moved beyond "protection" to embrace "asset privacy?"

Here's what I found out...

In America, 20% of lawyers do personal injury (in California there are 170,000 lawyers.) Only 1% do asset protection, and their primary strategy is a complex reactive maze of registered legal entities.

This event was held by a nationally known company. Since the early 1980s they advocate heavy duty use of Inc, LLC & LP structures. One client had 24 LLCs. Can you imagine that paperwork & fee nightmare? In my opinion, way overkill yet neither lawyer nor clients know there's anything else. They do not use or even mention business trusts.

EPILOGUE

I've been around a few years and have another perspective of what makes practical sense. I've done the corps, I've done the LLCs, and I've done the trusts. I know the real-world burden as both an advisor and principal. To me, these lawyers are selling big scare, you need us. It's a farce only to keep their hands on your 'soon to be' skinny wallet. Even worse, their registered business structures are easily found on the internet. Yet I can also understand how some people go with with their services because they don't know any better.

I do agree with them that C corporations are tremendously useful for operations and taxes. But you don't need a regular corporation. What you do need is corporate "tax classification," which is available with a business trust.

I would use an attorney for problems such as wrongful death or egregious fraud. But not for privacy protection. Their only mindset is battle, how to do versus how to avoid.

One attorney challenged those who recommend trusts for title to prove they defended someone in court. He missed my point, if you do it right there is no court; Defendants lose, plaintiffs lose but both attorneys always win fees. Lawsuits are a sticky spider's web. Stay out;

Despite the internet, lawyers and attorneys generally fail to recognize or explain the importance of asset privacy. I'm sure it would hurt their income. Meanwhile, client assets are visible targets. That's exactly the reason I'm writing this book. We use stealth for "title" to aircraft, bank account, real estate and businesses to stay clear of painful spiders and man-eating crocodiles.

The protection maze is a royal pain and I suspect few really understand what they're doing. The privacy alternative is simple to understand and sleep at night. It just makes common sense.

What strategy works best for you in 2018 – protection or privacy? Even if you want both, which naturally comes first?

– James,
February 27, 2018

EPILOGUE

ACKNOWLEDGEMENTS

Jack Miller taught me inspiration, perseverance, and attitude. He also introduced the importance of title and situs. David Johnston in Scotland led me to explore fideicommissa at the Vatican Library. And to Victor Hernandez, my dynamic co-writer in Mexico City, for bringing this book to life.

ACKNOWLEDGEMENTS

GLOSSARY

The following glossary contains terms that are relevant to
business trusts and to trusts in general. While some of the
terms may not appear in this book, they may appear in
situations that could be relevant to the use of a trust.

Anonymous – nameless, unidentified,
secret, unknown

Beneficial Interest – personal property rights

Beneficiary – person entitled to property rights for
their enjoyment

Beneficiary Agreement – description of
responsibilities or benefits

Blind – when trustees manage assets without
disclosure to the beneficiaries

Business – engaged in a for profit-seeking enterprise

Business Trust – a commercial enterprise formed

as a trust

Calendar Year – January through December

Charitable Remainder – Trust for retirement and estate planning

Chose in Action – right to go to law to obtain payment of money or damages

Commercial Trust – bargained for exchange or economic transaction. Examples include social security, ERISA, pensions, mutual funds, oil & gas royalty, law office trust account, bankruptcy, REITs

Common Law – originally English case law adopted by the US Constitution

Complex Trust – when trustee distributes principal or capital gains to beneficiaries

Contingency Fee – a form of payment agreement between an attorney and a plaintiff in which the attorney does not ask for payment up front. Instead, the attorney received a percent of the award granted by the court if the plaintiff wins the case

Corporation – traditional business structure authorized by the state to operate as a single entity for commercial purposes

Corporate Veil – a set of legal and fiscal benefits that protect the owners of a traditional business structure, such as corporation or LLC

Corporate Veil Piercing – the removal of the legal and fiscal benefits found in traditional business structures when the owners have failed followed the established rules and regulations

Declaration of Trust – oral or written contract that binds grantor, trustee and beneficiary to each other

Demise – to grant a lease in property

Devise – a gift made in a will

Director – person that gives instructions to the trustee in a realty trust

Domicile – where the trustee or beneficiary intends to legally reside with rights, duties and obligation

Equity – property interest or rights, use, equitable

ownership of a trust beneficiary

Escheat – reversion of land to the state by someone without a will

Express Trust – demonstrated by a written trust declaration

Fideicommissa – Roman law mechanism where testator charged an heir/trustee to act on behalf of a 3rd party

Fiduciary – a trusted relationship between a trustee and beneficiary

Fiscal Year – custom accounting year

Franchise Tax – a privilege tax collected by the state from a traditional business structure in order to operate in that state

Grant Deed – instrument that conveys realty title from a seller to a buyer

Grantor Trust – where all taxable items are recognized on the grantor's personal tax return

Grantor/Settlor/Creator – person that creates a trust

IN PERSONAM – lawsuit or proceeding against a person (individual)

IN REM – lawsuit or proceedings against a property or thing (ex, real estate)

INC – Incorporated. The term refers to a traditional corporation

Intestate – died without a will

Irrevocable – when grantor is unable to cancel, revoke or amend the trust. Typical of real estate and business trusts

Invisibility – when the information of an asset and its owner is not available to the public and it is difficult to obtain

Land Trust – in broader terms also known as Real Estate Trust. Holds real estate, mortgages, options, easements, leases, remainder estates, etc

Lien – a right to retain possession pending satisfaction of an obligation, often debt

Living Trust – also known as inter-vivos (Latin "between the living") to avoid probate and distribute estate.

LLC – Limited Liability Company. A traditional business structures that combines pass-through tax elements of partnership or sole proprietorship and the limited liability of a corporation

Pass through – fiscal treatment given to revenue from a business trust to a beneficiary if there is only one beneficiary. The business trust itself is not taxed. The single beneficiary is taxed on the pass through revenue

Partnership – business entity in which a group of people own and operate the business

Pension – holds salary and wage contributions for investment and protection

Personal Property – any property other than real estate

Personal Trust – gratuitous or gift from a donor, no exchange. examples include inter-vivos living, charitable, foundations, insurance

Principal – in business structures, a person who has ownership of the business structure

Privacy Curtain – a type of protection for assets in which the assets' ownership information is difficult to find because it is not publicly available. A privacy curtain gives invisibility to your assets

Qualified Sub S – holds shares of S corporation in private for a beneficiary

Real Estate Trust – in narrower terms also known as Land Trust. Holds real estate, mortgages, options, easements, leases, remainder interests, etc

REITS – Real Estate Investment Trusts. Companies that provide an investment structure similar to mutual funds through the use of income-producing real estate with special tax benefits

Remainder – residual interest reserved for someone when another person's estate ends

Reversion – a remainder interest which is created automatically by law

GLOSSARY

Revocable – this means grantor can cancel, revoke or amend the trust

Resident Agent – a legal representative who receiving service of process (legal action notices) for a corporation or LLC

Secretary of State – government agency that registers traditional business structures such as corporations and LLCs

Shared Equity – substitute for lease option to divide income/profits

Simple Trust – where trustee must distribute current income to beneficiaries

Situs – the place to which for purposes of legal jurisdiction or taxation, a property belongs

Small Business Trust (election) – internal revenue code for estate tax treatment of multiple beneficiaries related to S corporations

Sole proprietor – a business entity in which one natural person owns and operates the business

Statutory Law – set forth and authorized by specific statute law (state)

Successor Beneficiary – follows after the initial beneficiary

Successor Trustee – follows after the initial trustee.

Tax Classification – for a business structure, the fiscal treatment given by the IRS based on the way the business structure is arranged

Title – the ownership of an asset

Title Holding Trust – a tool for pending real estate transactions

Trust – An agreement for the administration of assets by a trustee for the benefit of a beneficiary

Trust Fund – setup to provide an income to beneficiaries

Trustee – holds legal and sometimes equitable title to an asset as fiduciary for a beneficiary

Trustee Agreement – powers authorized for a trustee

to act

UCC – uniform commercial code for securing personal property

Visibility – when the information of an asset and its owner is available to the public and it is easy to obtain

Wardship – lucrative right to act as guardian for a minor upon the death of the father

BIBLIOGRAPHY

Sources that informed the author on the subject of business trusts include, but are not limited to:

Maitland, F.W.. *State, Trust and Corporation*. Cambridge University Press, 2003.

Langbein, John H. *The Secret Life of the Trust: The Trust as an Instrument of Commerce*. Yale Law School Repository, 1997.

Luna., J.J.. *How to be Invisible*. St Martin's Press. Editorial de Las Islas LC, 2012.

Miller, Jack. *Advanced Corporate – Trust – LLC Strategies*. Cashflow Concepts LLC, 2002.

Johnston, David. *The Roman Law of Trusts*. Clarendon Press – Oxford, 1988.

Maitland, F.W.. *Equity*. Cambridge University Press, 1936.

BIBLIOGRAPHY

Watson, Alan. *The Law of Succession in the Later Roman Republic*. Clarendon Press – Oxford, 1972.

Bray, Judith. *A Student's Guide to Equity and Trusts*. Cambridge University Press, 2012.

Miller, Jack. *Advanced Trust Strategies*. Pacific Foundation Trust, 1997.

Bishop, Carter G. "Trusts, Taxes and Business". *Business Law Today*. American Bar Association. November, 2003.

Sitkoff, Robert H. *Trust as "Uncorporation": A Research Agenda*. University of Illinois Law Review, 2005.

Weissman, Michael L. *The Common law of Business Trusts*. Chicago-Kent Law Review, 1961.

Hansmann, Henry & Ugo Mattei. *Trust Law in the United States: A Basic Study of its Special Contribution*, UC Hastings College of Law, 1998.

Schwarcz, Steven L. *Commercial Trusts as Business Organizations: An Invitation to Comparatists*, Duke University Law School, April 2003.

INDEX

A

agency 60, 62

agreement 30, 60, 72

Alaska 82

Amazon 22

anonymity vii, xi, 44

antitrust 74

Apple 22

asset privacy xi, xii, 3, 9, 10, 15, 16, 54, 89, 91, 92

asset protection 66, 67, 82, 91

audit 33, 41

Australia 2

B

Bahamas 82

banking 2, 18, 19, 33-35, 63, 75, 85, 89

bankruptcy 22

beneficiary 16, 28, 40, 42, 51, 57-63, 66, 70-73, 75, 87

bifurcation 59, 62, 63

breadcrumb trail 25

brokerage 14, 28, 35, 53, 63, 67

business data hackers 44

business identity theft 46

business privacy 15, 54

business structures 1, 2, 7, 11, 17, 25, 27-29, 47, 48, 59, 74, 76, 80, 81, 85, 88, 92

business trust 2, 5, 13, 14, 16, 27-31, 33-55, 57-59, 62,

63, 65, 67, 69, 73-79, 81, 83, 85-89, 91, 92

C

California 11, 18, 20, 35-38, 40, 51, 91

capital 42, 48

Carnegies 2

certificate of good standing 34

civil judgment 25, 47, 48

Colorado 52

Common Law 29, 30, 71

Cook Islands 82

corporate identity theft 3, 46

corporate lawyer 50, 78

corporate structure 14, 21, 23, 25, 30, 31, 39, 62, 63, 75

corporate theft 46

corporate veil 11, 21-23, 33, 39, 41, 46, 47, 50, 51, 62

Courts of Chancery 73

Crown 71-73

Crusader 71

Crusades 71

D

database 18, 19, 23, 25, 29, 31, 38, 51

declaration 50

default judgment 25

default mindset 14

default option 79, 80

defensive 23, 82

Delaware 30, 82

director meetings 19

directors 19

domicile 28, 29

Dukes 72

E

EIN 34, 50, 63, 64, 87

England 71, 73

English Magna Carta 72

equity 66, 71

escrow 48

extortion 25, 50

F

feoffee 71

feoffor 71

feudal 71, 72

fideicommissa 15, 70, 95

fiduciary 58, 61, 62

finance 13, 29, 73, 79

financial privacy vii, 3

financial protections 75

financial theft 3

Fox News 86

franchise tax 19, 20, 22, 30, 35-38, 40, 54, 75, 79

Franciscan Friars 72

fraudulent 11, 46

G

German Civil Code 70

golden age of surveillance 25

Google 22, 24, 25, 43

gossips 44

grantor 57, 58, 75

H

hackers 44, 54

handicaps 6, 30, 52-54

heir 70, 72

Henry VIII 72

holding title 5, 12, 67, 73, 75

Hong Kong 2

I

identity theft 3, 44, 46

income 20, 36, 39-42, 78, 79, 92

India 2

inheritance 70, 77

insurance 43, 45-47, 70, 77

internal revenue code 6

internet vii, xii, 3, 11, 18, 23-25, 76, 81, 92

invisibility 35, 43, 75

invisible vii, 2, 14, 29, 31, 45

invisible title 14, 29

IRS 34, 39, 41, 42, 50, 63, 87

ITIN 87

J

Japan 2

K

Kennedys 2

King 71, 72

Kintner rules 40

L

landowner 71

lawsuit 21, 23, 25, 33, 43, 44,

48, 49, 62, 66, 92
legal extortion 25, 50
legal protections 18, 41, 62, 82
Lex Voconia 70
liability 11, 21, 30, 58, 59, 76
liability protections 11, 21, 30, 76
lien 25, 47, 48
litigation 3, 23, 33, 46, 48
living trust 27, 52, 77, 87
LLC xi, 1, 2, 11, 13, 14, 16-18, 20, 24, 28-30, 33, 34, 36-38, 43-46, 48-51, 59, 62, 63, 65, 67, 75, 76, 78-80, 82, 87, 91, 92
London 86
Lord Chancellor 71

M
majority stockholder 63
Malibu 11
Massachusetts 30
media 44
mega-rich 2
member shares 59
mentality 80-82

Merrill Lynch 35
Middle Ages 15, 71
monastery 72
monopolistic behavior 74
monopoly 74
Murdoch 2, 86
mutual funds 29, 73

N
name conflict 51, 52
naturalization 20, 29, 37, 45
Nevada 82
nobility 72
nosy people 44, 54

O
offensive setup 83
officer meetings 19
one-way mirror 31
opportunists 55

P
partnership 11, 17, 18, 40, 82, 87
penalties 6, 22, 39
Pepperdine 10
personal assets 22, 48, 62,

65

personal information 30, 34, 63, 64, 80

phony lawsuit 25

piercing the corporate veil 11, 21, 23

portability 45, 75, 76, 85

portable situs 29

principal 9, 11, 60, 92

privacy vii, xi, xii, 1-3, 9, 10, 12-16, 24-26, 29, 30, 35, 38, 40, 43-45, 51, 54, 55, 63, 65, 66, 73, 76, 78, 81-83, 85, 88, 89, 91-93

privacy curtain xii, 2, 10, 13, 14, 16, 25, 30, 35, 43-45, 54, 55, 73, 82, 83, 85, 89

private 13, 14, 16, 27, 31, 34, 66, 70, 73

proactive 77, 81-83

probated 63

public 11, 17, 18, 23, 29-31, 53, 55, 73, 79

R

reactive 77, 79-82, 91

reactive mentality 77, 79-82

realty trust law 71

recordkeeping 19, 47

red tape 18, 20, 47

regulations 2, 3, 12, 18, 21, 34, 47, 53

REIT 69, 79

renewal fees 79

resident agent 19, 20, 22, 23, 25, 36, 37, 44, 65, 78

restart insurance 47

revenue 6, 20, 34, 73

risk 1, 10, 11, 17, 18, 21, 23, 25, 26, 29, 33, 41, 43, 45-48, 59, 65, 71, 75, 80, 81, 83, 85, 87, 88

Rockefeller 2, 74

Romans 70, 87

Rome 15

Rupert Murdoch 86

S

Sam⑤Club 2

savings 35, 85

S corporation 40

Scottrade 35

Secretary of State 2, 11, 14, 17-20, 23-25, 30, 34, 36-

38, 44, 51, 54, 65, 75, 79, 89

serf 71, 72

shareholder 17-19, 22, 23, 28, 41, 50, 59, 62, 63, 67

shares 59, 72

Singapore 2

situs 9, 14, 27-29, 49, 83, 95

Social Security 34, 63, 73

sole proprietors 11, 17

SSN 87

Standard Oil 74

state database 25

state fees 35

state name conflicts 52

state portability 45, 85

Statutes of Mortmain 72

statutory 29, 30, 36, 75, 79

statutory business trust 29, 30, 36, 75, 79

stealth 33, 35, 63, 75, 83, 85, 89, 93

stockholder 17, 18, 22, 23, 28, 59, 60, 62, 63, 67

T

target for lawsuits 23, 62

target for opportunists 55

taxes 1, 5, 16, 18-20, 22, 25, 30, 33, 35-42, 47, 48, 54, 66, 71, 72, 75, 79, 92

Tax Reform (2018) 41, 93

tech security 54

testator 70

title 5, 9, 10, 12-16, 27-29, 58, 60, 67, 71-73, 75, 92, 93, 95

title and situs 9, 14, 27, 95

title holding trusts 12

title privacy 13, 15

traditional business structure 1, 2, 11, 17, 28, 29, 47, 48, 59, 80, 81, 85

traditional corporate structure 14, 21, 23, 30, 31, 39, 62, 63, 75

Treasury Regulations 301.7701 53

Treuhand 70

trust 2, 5, 10, 12-16, 27-31, 33-55, 57-65, 67, 69-79, 81, 83, 85-89, 91, 92

trustee 28, 29, 34, 45, 50, 51, 57-64, 70-73, 75, 87

trust fund 70, 73, 78
trustor 57, 58, 70

U
UK 2, 15
ultra high net worth 9
uncorporation 2, 39, 89
United States 18, 28, 30, 73
unlisted 30, 31, 38, 45, 48-
    50, 67, 75, 78, 79, 81, 83,
    86

V
Vatican Library 15, 95
veil piercing 21, 41
visibility 11, 79
visible 11, 14, 18, 23, 28, 92

W
Wall Street Journal 86
WalMart 2, 22, 86
Waltons 2, 86
wealth 2, 3, 15, 29, 30, 73, 75
wealthy 2, 9, 75
Wells Fargo 35

Made in the USA
Las Vegas, NV
09 October 2022

56865039R00080